I0530439

ORGANIC

ORGANIC

Copyright © 2024 by Ciara Dove
Riverdrive Publishing
All rights reserved

ISBN: 979-8-9923676-1-4

Visit me on the web!
www.CiaraDove.com

Produced by Publish Pros | publishpros.com

No portion of this book may be reproduced, stored in a retrieval
system, or transmitted in any form by any means–electronic,
mechanical, photo-copy, recording, or other–except for brief quotations
in printed reviews, without prior permission of the author.

ORGANIC

Poetry in the Raw...

Dedicated to...

The man that had me run alongside him in 90° weather.
The man that taught me how to fight,
trying to make me a boxer.
The man that encouraged me to be the warrior I am today.
I love you, Daddy!

- Cici

Prologue

Welcome back to the 2nd book of the Poetry in the Raw series. Now that you've seen my process and style of writing poetry in its rawest form, I invite you to open up and continue to dive deeper into yourself as I lift the veil to my heart and soul. Diving into oneself requires profoundly facing harsh truths and is not for the faint-hearted.

Through *ORGANIC*, I'm searching for myself and what makes me happy. Well, in this case, I'm looking for the 'whom' and how they could make me happy. While trying to figure out what is the best avenue for my family, I jeopardize my own happiness through unfolding developments.

Still in chronological order, you will see the progression of life, lust, and the affairs of mixed emotions with the turn of each page. As I get more seasoned in life's experiences with the twists and turns of events depicting a roller coaster effect; there are emergences of subliminal addictions, annoyances, and some lustful loves that could be misconstrued as infatuation.

During this time, it felt like I needed to hurdle obstructions, while jerking my tears to make me stronger and get through turmoil. I didn't realize that in the same token, I was creating my own demise.

Enough said!
Hold my hand as we take a plunge deeper into the exposures of my vulnerability.

The Essence

Open your mind to the revelations of the heart. 🩶

◇ Mark your favorites here, as you go!

Poetry in the Raw...

Rebuilding

I'm tired of wallowing in self-pity
It's just getting me no where
from the lack of sleep at night
To having puffy eyes from so many tears

It's time I find myself
And stop dwelling in a negative past
Start being more self sufficient
This I know, will be no easy task

First I need to start inside
Then work my way out
Believe and trust in myself
And never have one inch or ounce of doubt.

Some may say that was my downfall
To harbor low self esteem
But as I work on myself inside & out
I will soon have limitless dreams

2

Rebuilding

I'm tired of wallowing in self-pity
It's just getting me no where
From the lack of sleep at night
To having puffy eyes from so many tears

It's time I find myself
And stop dwelling in a negative past
Start being more self-sufficient
This I know, will be no easy task

First, I need to start inside
Then work my way out
Believe and trust in myself
And never have one inch or ounce of doubt

Some may say that was my downfall
To harbor low self-esteem
But as I work on myself inside and out
I will soon have limitless dreams

Patience III.

If he was meant for you
He will come back no matter what
In the meantime, stay focused on what you need to do
And God will deliver him to you, with perfect love & trust

Never question the love he has for you
As it will make you craze
Think about the good times he's shared with you
And you'll see the results will be amazing

The results of true love
The results of you two, meaning to be
The results with God's help from above
Give it time and patience and you will see

4

Patience 111

If he was meant for you
He will come back no matter what
In the meantime, stay focused on what you need to do
And God will deliver him to you; with perfect love and trust

Never question the love he has for you
As it will make you crazy
Think about the good times he's shared with you
And you'll see, the results will be amazing

The results of true love
The results of you two, meaning to be
The results with God's help from above
Give it time and patience and you will see

Valentine's Day

Today is lovers day
And I'm spending it alone
I chose for it to be this way
As I don't want my unhappiness shown

Although I was so down
He called and lifted me up
Invited me out first thing for chow
This is my day and not by luck

Overwhelmed by his invitation
I felt compelled to do something special
So I got him a card & signed to it my famous inscription
Forever Always, my love is unconditional

Valentine's Day

Today is lovers' day
And I'm spending it alone
I chose for it to be this way
As I don't want my unhappiness shown

Although I was so down
He called and lifted me up
Invited me out, first thing for chow
This is my day and not by luck

Overwhelmed by his invitation
I felt compelled to do something special
So, I got him a card and signed to it my famous inscription
Forever always, my love is unconditional

Accept me as I am

Accept me as I am
Take me as your whole
I'm prepared to be your wife
To have forever and to hold

Accept me as I am
As I am ready to make that change
Please take my heart, my love & everything
And I'll take yours in exchange

Accept me as I am
We musn't waste anymore time
Time waits for no one
So lets not watch it go by.

8

Accept Me as I Am

Accept me as I am
Take me as your whole
I'm prepared to be your wife
To have forever and to hold

Accept me as I am
As I am ready to make that change
Please take my heart, my love and everything
And I'll take yours in exchange

Accept me as I am
We mustn't waste any more time
Time waits for no one
So, let's not watch it go by

The Other Woman

I have so much anger
I have so much rage
my only escape was my dreams

now as I lay me down to rest
my safe haven has been interrupted
my place of escape is now a mystery

Interrupted by thoughts of him & her
And how I can't stand her right now
For thinking she can just move in on my family

I'm franchise I aint going no where
you can deal with it or just leave
I would much rather you leave of course

Leave me and my family alone
Return to your ever-so fulfilled life
cause this man is my man and can't be bought

Find your own man
stop preying on mine
Perhaps three is not your charm

First engaged   (man #1)
Second engaged to be (man #2)
Third is my man, not for you but for me

10

The Other Woman

I have so much anger
I have so much rage
My only escape is my dreams

Now as I lay me down to rest
My safe haven has been interrupted
My place of escape is now a mystery

Interrupted by thoughts of him and her
And how I can't stand her right now
For thinking she can just move in on my family

I'm franchise, I aint going no where
You can deal with it or just leave
I would much rather you leave, of course

Leave me and my family alone
Return to your ever-so fulfilled life
Cause this man is my man and can't be bought

Find your own man
Stop preying on mine
Perhaps three is not your charm

First engaged (man #1)
Second engaged to be (man #2)
Third is my man, not for you, but for me

False Hope ✓

Haven't had the time to write
* As I've been so happy and proud
Proud to be together as a family again
* And not ashamed to scream it aloud

Scream it to the heavens
* Tell   it to whomever is near
Scream it to the top of my lungs
* Tell you that I've missed you so much my dear

Thank you for humbling yourself
* Thank you for giving us another try
What is this you're speaking of contradiction
* I knew this was coming and I promised myself not to cry

You've practiced this humility thing all too well
* I knew it was too good to be true
Staying over all night playing me, Love
* Only to tell me 4 days later, "this can't continue"

Continue, it will not
* Although your actions speak otherwise
I will give you your space
* As you wish, I will oblige

12

False Hope

Haven't had the time to write
As I've been so happy and proud
Proud to be together as a family again
And not ashamed to scream it aloud

Scream it to the heavens
Tell it to whomever is near
Scream it to the top of my lungs
Tell you that I've missed you so much my dear

Thank you for humbling yourself
Thank you for giving us another try
What is this you're speaking of contradiction?
I knew this was coming and I promised myself not to cry

You've practiced this humility thing all too well
I knew it was too good to be true
Staying over all night playing Mr. Lover
Only to tell me four days later, 'this can't continue'

Continue, it will not
Although your actions speak otherwise
I will give you your space
As you wish; I will oblige

3/4/08
9:31pm

His Plans to Stay...

Can't you see the tone on my face
Can't you hear the look in my tone
It's asking you to stay at my place
Begging you to make this house your home

I can tell you don't want to leave
Because you're very hesitant to go
I can also tell that you're waiting on me
To give you a quick yes or a simple no

Instead I left it up to you
Gave you the opportunity to come back
By putting minimal to no pressure on you
Let's see if my plan works precise & exact

14

His Plans to Stay...

Can't you see the tone on my face?
Can't you hear the look in my tone?
It's asking you to stay at my place
Begging you to make this house your home

I can tell you don't want to leave
Because you're very hesitant to go
I can also tell that you're waiting on me
To give you a quick yes, or a simple no

Instead, I left it up to you
Gave you the opportunity to come back
By putting minimal to no pressure on you
Let's see if my plan works precise and exact

3/5/08
11:11 pm

... where plans to leave
my plan did not work
* At least tonight it didn't
Lets see how things play out tomorrow
* As the presence of love is evident

Today is now tomorrow
* The night of day I spoke of yesterday
He said that he'll be back ouch
* But I guess not tonight; at least not to stay

So I'll wait for him another night
* And another after that
Until he's ready to stay ouch
* Or ash me to come back

16

...Were Plans to Leave

My plan did not work
At least tonight it didn't
Let's see how things play out tomorrow
As the presence of love is evident

Today is now tomorrow
The night of day I spoke of yesterday
He said that he'll be back over
But I guess not tonight; at least not to stay

So, I'll wait for him another night
And another after that
Until he's ready to stay over
Or ask me to come back

3/6/08

Confidence

He may be the indecisive one
But I already know what I want us to become

He may be cautious this time
But I have intentions on making him mine

He may not want to take the next step
But I'm here to change his mind about that

Confidence

He may be the indecisive one
But I already know what I want us to become

He may be cautious this time
But I have intentions on making him mine

He may not want to take the next step
But I'm here to change his mind about that

3/6/08 ~ 1
   8:50pm   ✓

                  You don't know what you have
All this time I've wasted
On what couldve been eternally mine
All this energy I've wasted
On trying to be angry all the time

I felt I still had love for him
But I chose to do my own thing
The old habits of when we were first an item
                    now
Are ^coming out as a natural instinct

20

You Don't Know What You Have...

All this time I've wasted
On what could've been eternally mine
All this energy I've wasted
On trying to be angry all the time

I felt I still had love for him
But I chose to do my own thing
The old habits of when we were first an item
Are now coming out as a natural instinct

3/6/08 -2
6:01pm   ✓

...until it's gone
He speaks with a certain tongue
* That makes me think about our past
I've always said he is full of wisdom
* yet his Reality I can't seem to grasp

I'm trying ~~sometimes~~ to humble myself
* not for his sake but for my own
It's working for me thus far
* AS I don't want to end up alone

my predecessor's downfall was; not listening
* I don't want that to be my legacy
I'd like to be the one to make that change
* As I have children I want to look up to me

22

...Until It's Gone

He speaks with a certain tongue
That makes me think about our past
I've always said he is full of wisdom
Yet his reality I can't seem to grasp

I'm trying to humble myself
Not for his sake, but for my own
It's working for me thus far
As I don't want to end up alone

My predecessor's downfall was not listening
I don't want that to be my legacy
I'd like to be the one to make that change
As I have children, I want to look up to me

3/11/08
4:08pm

Reminiscing

I'm sitting here at work with a smile
on my face
Awaiting to come home to feel your warm
embrace

I can't help but to reminisce about the
past
And all the inside jokes that made us
laugh

The more I think about the way we
were
The more I think of how it was so
much easier

Reminiscing

I'm sitting here at work with a smile on my face
Awaiting to come home to feel your warm embrace

I can't help but to reminisce about the past
And all the inside jokes that made us laugh

The more I think about the way we were
The more I think of how it was so much easier

3/7/08 -1
11:59 pm   ✓

Being   Untrue
I'm so hurt inside and out
But my pain you will never see
I've loved you for a long time withouta doubt
But I can't continue to be the person you want me to be

I've been unfaithful for a long time
So much it feels like second nature
I found myself telling lie after lie
For someone in which I had no future

your way of camouflaging your infidelity
Is to be invective toward others
By making them feel inadequate & full of uncertainty
Even if they were once your lover

26

Being Untrue

I'm so hurt, inside and out
But my pain you will never see
I've loved you for a long time, without a doubt
But I can't continue to be the person you want me to be

I've been unfaithful for a long time
So much, it feels like second nature
I found myself telling lie after lie
For someone in which I had no future

Your way of camouflaging your infidelity
Is to be invective toward others
By making them feel inadequate and full of uncertainty
Even if they were once your lover

3/9/08
4:00pm

Who I Am

If you really know me
Then you'll know the type of person I am
When I love, I love whole heartedly
not with conditions due to circumstance

I'm known to be a very forgiving person
Which tends to be misconstrued as being naive
I get mad at myself when I try to change that person
As I know this is the person I'm designed to be

The forgiving one
The loving seed
The understanding one
who's always there in time of need

Who I Am

If you really know me
Then you'll know the type of person I am
When I love, I love whole heartedly
Not with conditions due to circumstance

I'm known to be a very forgiving person
Which tends to be misconstrued as being naïve
I get mad at myself when I try to change that person
Even though this is the person I'm designed to be

The forgiving one
The loving seed
The understanding one
Who's always there, in time of need

3/9/08
4:19 pm ✓

Forgive & Forget

She was always on my mind
* Different and most times of the day
This time a little more than usual
* Enough for her to call and reach out to say:

"I know it's been a while
* And I'm sorry for hurting you
But if you can find it in your heart to forgive me
* I'll be just around the corner from you"

30

Forgive & Forget

She was always on my mind
Different and most times of the day
This time a little more than usual
Enough for her to call and reach out to say:

I know its been a while
And I'm sorry for hurting you
But if you can find it in your heart to forgive me
I'll be just around the corner from you

3/9/08 - 1
4:50 pm   ✓

Addicted

They say crack is wack
But I feel the urge to go back

not back for a fix
Back because, you I miss

The person you are inside
The person I try so hard to deny

Deny everything and all you stand for
I've opened pandora's box and now can't seem to
close the door.

Addicted

They say crack is wack
But I feel the urge to go back

Not back for a fix
Back because it's you, I miss

The person you are inside
The person I try so hard to deny

Deny everything and all you stand for
I've opened Pandora's box, and now can't seem to close the door

3/11/08 ✓

PRESSURE

I don't know what to do
Cause now I really have to come through

I am so stressed out
Everyone can see it without a doubt

This pressure is consuming me
To the point where I can't even sleep

no sleep, no food
no love, bad mode

34

Pressure

I don't know what to do
Cause now, I really have to come through

I am so stressed out
Everyone can see it without a doubt

This pressure is consuming me
To the point where I can't even sleep

No sleep, no food
No love, bad mood

3/11/08
      5:50 pm   ✓

                    missed calls

you don't call me anymore
Should I even care
I've been trying to let go for the longest
But now I miss you more and wish you were here

I called you like crazy today
To the point where it would be an annoyance
I guess you weren't there to answer
                  at all
Or even make a cameo appearance

yea I still use your phrases
Hope you don't mind
I wish things were different between us
If we could only turn back the hands of time

Missed Calls

You don't call me anymore
Should I even care?
I've been trying to let go for the longest
But now I miss you more, and wish you were here

I called you like crazy today
To the point where it would be an annoyance
I guess you weren't there at all to answer
Or even make a "cameo appearance"

Yea, I still use your phrases
Hope you don't mind
I wish things were different between us
If we could only turn back the hands of time

3/19/08
   5:55pm

Withdrawal

subject [I'm going through withdrawal]
I haven't written in days
Haven't slept in ~~almost~~ ~~2~~ weeks
Have no appetite for food
And no desire to eat

subject [I'm sleep deprived]
I go to bed thinking about you
I wake up thinking about us
my thoughts consumed by all we've been through
And how we're going to rebuild this trust

subject [I'm curious and concerned]
③ I'm curious to know what will come of this
② As you've put our relationship on display
① The privacy of our home no larger exists
④ And concerned how things are going to change
day-to-day

Withdrawal

'I'm going through withdrawal'

I haven't written in days
Haven't slept in weeks
Have no appetite for food
And no desire to eat

'I'm sleep deprived'

I go to bed thinking about you
I wake up thinking about us
My thoughts consumed by all we've been through
And how we're going to rebuild this trust

'I'm curious and concerned'

The privacy of our home no longer exists
As you've put our relationship on display
I'm curious to know what will become of this
And concerned how things are going to change day-to-day

3/22/08
4:24pm

PRIORITIES

you're home now
How does it feel
you hungry baby
want me to make you a meal

Yea you're home now
who's the first person you wanna see
cause it damn sure aint your child
Or else you would've seen her this morning

you spent 2 hours with me
And 7-hours with your friends
Did either one of them ask if you've seen
your child
Or spent any time with your girlfriend

no probably not
cause we're last on your list
you know you're coming home to us
So how much is there to miss

40

Priorities

You're home now.
How does it feel?
You hungry, baby?
Want me to make you a meal?

Yea you're home now
Who's the first person you want to see?
Because it damn sure aint your child
Or else you would've seen her this morning

You've spent two hours with me
And seven hours with your friends
Did either one of them ask if you've seen your child
Or spent any time with your girlfriend?

No, probably not
Because we're last on your list
You know you're coming home to us
So how much is there to miss?

3/24/08
5:46pm

fasting

If he can't eat
neither will I

If he can't sleep
neither will I ?

If he cries every night
So will I

And prays with all his might
So will I

If he turns over a new leaf
I will do the same

Together we will both succeed
This I will and I do proclaim

Fasting

If he can't eat
Neither will I

If he can't sleep
Neither will I

If he cries every night
So will I

And prays with all his might
So will I

If he turns over a new leaf
I will do the same

Together we will both succeed
This I will, and I do proclaim

3/26/08
4:29 pm   ✓
                    Undeniable feeling

Do I love you?
Or am I stringing you along
maybe you were convenient at the time
The time where the other was gone

now that the other is back
I'm a little hesitant to let you go
As I may need you later on down the line
for financial needs, not so much the physical

I'm sorry to be so honest
But I have no reason to lie
I shouldn't be talking to you in the first place
But the feelings in my heart I can't deny

I wish I could let you go for good
And erase the feelings I have in my heart
you aren't making this easy for me
As I wanted to end this from the start

44

Undeniable Feeling

Do I love you,
Or am I stringing you along?
Maybe you were convenient at the time
The time where the other was gone

Now that the other is back
I'm a little hesitant to let you go
As I may need you later on down the line
For financial needs, not so much the physical

I'm sorry to be so honest
But I have no reason to lie
I shouldn't be talking to you in the first place
But the feelings in my heart, I can't deny

I wish I could let you go for good
And erase these feelings I have in my heart
You aren't making this easy for me
As I wanted to end this from the start

3/28/08

Essential

my love is to your heart
what your heart is to my soul

my time is to your existence
what your time is to my being

my goals are to your dreams
what your dreams are to my happiness

Essential

My love is to your heart
What your heart is to my soul

My time is to your existence
What your time is to my being

My goals are to your dreams
What your dreams are to my happiness

Essential

5/30/08

The Bond

~~no matter what~~

no matter what
I wont stop believing in you

no matter what
I'll stick by you through and through

no matter what
our time will come

no matter what
we'll be united as one

no matter whom
will come in our way

no matter whom
we will turn them away

no matter whom
may dislike us

no matter whom
may despise us

48

The Bond

No matter what
I won't stop believing in you

No matter what
I'll stick by you, through and through

No matter what
Our time will come

No matter what
We'll be united as one

No matter who
Will come in our way

No matter whom
We will turn them away

No matter who
May dislike us

No matter who
May despise us

we will always come together
And be that way forever

continued

We will always come together
And be that way, forever

✓

Interrogatively Pronouncing

Who	Who will stand by you just as I have?
What	What would they've done if I hadn't?
When	When would be the right time to discuss our future?
Where	Where would this moment take place?
Why	Why can't we see the strength of our love?
How	How do we keep it and maintain it? (adjective)

The Answer

P.S.N.Y.E.R.

Interrogatively Pro-Nouning

Who will stand by you just as I have?
What would they have done if I hadn't?
When would be the right time to discuss our future?
Where would this moment take place?
Why can't we see the strength of our love?
How do we keep it and maintain it?

P.R.A.Y.E.R.

3/31/08
5:36pm

/

Goodbye

You make it too easy for me to let go
By slandering the people I know

You think we've been through so much together
But yet we have a bigger storm to weather

The storm of each other
And the discontinuation of us being lovers

I can control the storm's path
But can you handle the aftermath

This is my goodbye to you
I hope you have a good future too

As it will not include me in it
But our love for each other will remain infinite

Goodbye FoREVER

54

Goodbye

You make it so easy for me to let go
By slandering the people I know

You think we've been through so much together
But yet we have a bigger storm to weather

The storm of each other
And the discontinuation of us being lovers

I can control the storm's path
But can you handle the aftermath?

This is my goodbye to you
I hope you have a good future too

As it will not include me in it
But our love for each other will remain infinite

Goodbye Forever.

4/11/08 5:47pm

Cliché's

An apple a day keeps the dr. away
Or so they say

Some vitamin C and some protein will
keep you lean
Or so it seems?

So I say to you...

A simple "I love you" a day will
keep the stress away

A simple "I miss you" a day will
keep your heart from going astray

Clichés

An apple a day keeps the doctor away
Or so they say

Some vitamin C and some protein will keep you lean
Or so it seems

So, I say to you…

A simple, *'I love you'* a day
Will keep the stress away

A simple, *'I miss you'* a day
Will keep your heart from going astray

4/2/08
5:50pm
PREPARATIONS

I love you
But I love me more
I'm putting my life on hold
Pending a decision or score

If things rule in your favor
should I prepare for a celebration
of a positive outcome and new life
of greater and higher expectations

If things turn out the opposite
what are you going to expect from me
wait for you until everything is over
or ask me to continue my life and be free

It may be a bit early to ask these questions
But I think it's only fair to your daughter & I
would you be so selfish and ask us to wait
or would you suggest we go on with our lives

58

Preparations

I love you
But I love me more
I'm putting my life on hold
Pending a decision or score

If things rule in your favor
Should I prepare for a celebration?
Of a positive outcome and new life
Of greater and higher expectations

If things turn out the opposite
What are you going to expect from me?
Wait for you until everything is over
Or ask me to continue my life and be free?

It may be a bit early to ask these questions
But I think it's only fair to your daughter and I
Would you be so selfish, and ask us to wait
Or would you suggest we go on with our lives?

4/3/08
5:59pm   ✓

Don't Ride the 5o'clock Train

I'm surrounded by filth and germs
* not much ventilation coming inside or out
Gasping for even a wiff of fresh air
People sneezing, coughing, and blowing oss aloud

How much longer do I have to put up with this
* Cause I'm ready to burn all of my clothing
Wash my hair and scrub my body
* As this daily routine is getting tired/annoying.

Whom ever created this way to save money
* was very smart in their invention
Too bad they didn't come up with a way to
sanitize it
* This damn thing we call, Public Transpartation

Don't Ride the five o'clock
                    train

Don't Ride the 5 o' Clock Train

I'm surrounded by filth and germs
Not much ventilation coming inside or out
Gasping for even a whiff of fresh air
People sneezing, coughing and blowing ass aloud

How much longer do I have to put up with this?
Because I'm ready to burn all my clothing
Wash my hair, and scrub my body
As this daily routine is getting tired and annoying

Whoever created this way to save money
Was very smart in their invention
Too bad they didn't come up with a way to sanitize it
This damn thing we call public transportation

4/4/08

6-years

Today marks the 2,190th day of our relationship
which makes this a special day
I wish I felt that in my mind or in my heart
But I honestly don't feel any type of way

A card of some sort
To show a thoughtful gesture
A hug, a kiss, a smile ... something
Anything to make me feel secure

Thanks for making this day special for me
Just as I've done for you
I know you've got a lot on your mind
But don't you think I do too

You aren't in this alone
What you go through I do too
But Lets not lose touch with our romantic side
And keep our love in tact as we know it to
be true

62

6 Years

Today marks the 2,190th day of our relationship
Which makes this a special day
I wish I felt that in my mind, or in my heart
But I honestly don't feel any type of way

A card of some sort
To show a thoughtful gesture
A hug, a kiss, a smile…something
Anything to make me feel secure

Thanks for making this day special for me
Just as I've done for you
I know you've got a lot on your mind
But don't you think I do too

You aren't in this alone
What you go through, I do too
But let's not lose touch with our romantic side
And keep our love intact, as we know it to be true

4/9/08

Exhausting Affair

I love him
And he loves me
But his love goes deeper
And further than the eye can see

I'm like a light switch
I can turn it on and off
As his love and needs progress
I have reached the point of exhaust

I'm tired of this love affair
As that is all it is
But he sees nothing wrong with it
And would rather continue this charade of bliss

1 I have a family at home
2 That I need to take care of
② Just as he does
3 And I want to give them my undivided
   attention [4] and my unconditional love

How can he compete
As he is of no comparison
The love for my ole man will remain the same
And only for that one person

64

Exhausting Affair

I love him
And he loves me
But his love goes deeper
And farther than the eye can see

I'm like a light switch
I can turn it on and off
As his love and needs progress
I have reached the point of exhaust

I'm tired of this love affair
As that is all it is
But he sees nothing wrong with it
And would rather continue this charade of bliss

I have a family at home
Just as he does, that I need to take care of
And I want to give them my undivided attention
And my unconditional love

How can he compete?
As he is of no comparison
The love for my ole man will remain the same
And only for that one person

4/15/08
8:33am ✓

Deeply In Love

I miss you so much
So much that I haven't slept
Haven't slept in so long
So long that I can't function
Can't function with out hearing your voice
Hearing your voice in my head
In my head you will always remain
Always remain in my thoughts
In my thoughts I just can't stop
Can't stop making love to you
To you and all the things we used to do
Used to do to and for one another
For one another we will never need any other

66

Deeply In Love

I miss you so much
So much I haven't slept
Haven't slept in so long
So long that I can't function
Can't function without hearing your voice
Hearing your voice in my head
In my head you will always remain
Always remain in my thoughts
In my thoughts I just can't stop
Can't stop making love to you
To you and all the things we used to do
Used to do to and for one another
For one another we will never need any other

4/16/08

Are you mad

Are you mad at me
Are you mad that I still call you
Are you mad that I just call to hear
your voice
Are you mad that I block my number
when I call
Are you mad because I mute my phone
so you don't hear my breathing
Are you mad that I can't get over you?

68

Are You Mad?

Are you mad at me?
Are you mad that I still call you?
Are you mad that I just call to hear your voice?
Are you mad that I block my number when I call?
Are you mad because I mute my phone, so you don't hear me breathing?
Are you mad that I can't get over you?

4/16/08 ✓

Thinking of you

You're in my thoughts
You're in my dreams
Everyday at 4 o'clock in the morning

② While I'm still awake
① I'm struggling to call you
③ 'cause in my mind, I see your face

Why have I abandoned you?
Why did I put you through this pain?
Because we have a love that can't be explained

I'll always love you
And treasure every moment
I just wish we had more time together spent

Thinking of You

You're in my thoughts
You're in my dreams
Every day at 4 o' clock in the morning

I'm struggling to call you
While I'm still awake
Cause in my mind, I see your face

Why have I abandoned you?
Why did I put you through this pain?
Because we have a love that can't be explained

I'll always love you
And treasure every moment
I just wish we had more time together, spent

4/17/08
am

Choose

Is it bipolarism
Or is it indecisiveness
Can't seem to make up your mind
On whether you want stress or happiness

One minute you're up
Confident as hell
Next moment you're down
         Shattered like a glass shell

Take your time
Take things as they come
While you're ignoring happiness
         The stress will make you numb

Choose

Is it bi-polarism,
Or is it indecisiveness?
Can't seem to make up your mind
On whether you want stress or happiness

One minute you're up
Confident as hell
Next moment you're down
Shattered like a glass shell

Take your time
Take things as they come
While you're ignoring happiness
The stress will make you numb

4/17/08

One Response ~~needed~~

I feel better if you know how I feel for you
Don't respond ...

I feel better when I email you and get no reply
Don't respond ...

I feel better when I read our last correspondence
Don't respond ...

I feel better knowing that you've checked my message
Don't respond ...

I feel better hearing your voice & you hearing mine
Don't respond ...

I'd feel better if you said yes to one having lost time
PLEASE respond ...

One Response

I feel better, if you know how I feel for you
Don't respond…

I feel better, when I email you and get no reply
Don't respond…

I feel better, when I read our last email correspondence
Don't respond…

I feel better, knowing that you've checked my messages
Don't respond…

I feel better, hearing your voice and you hearing mine
Don't respond…

I'd feel better, if you said yes to having one last time
Please respond.

4/21/08   ✓

                    Mr. Robinson
        I saw him on the train
        He looked a lot like my first love
        The side profile of his face
        Recalling his voice saying my name, dave

        To my surprise it wasn't him
Though I shouldn't expect to find him here
        As he's in another state married w/twins
        So in my heart he shall remain near and dear.

        P.S. ~~miss you much.~~
                ~~Sir Robinson~~

76

Mr. Robinson

I saw him on the train
He looked a lot like my first love
The side profile of his face
Recalling his voice, saying my name, 'Dove'

To my surprise, it wasn't him
Though I shouldn't expect to find him here
As he's in another state, married with twins
So, in my heart, he shall remain near and dear

4/21/08 ✓

Flirting at The Deli

Since I've been coming here
We've never spoke
At least not like we want to
So instead we exchange jokes

② Enjoying the food he's prepared
① I sit and dine-in
④ As I'm Eating away giving an occasional stare
③ we grab each others attention

78

Flirting at the Deli

Since I've been coming here
We've never spoke
At least not like we want to
So instead, we exchange jokes

I sit, and dine-in
Enjoying the food he's prepared
We grab each other's attention
As I'm eating away, giving an occasional stare

Wandering Thoughts

I'm here with him
But thinking of you
This just isn't right
But what else am I to do

Is this deception?
I feel disgraced
I just miss you so much
And miss seeing your face

Would I be this way?
If you were available
Would I want to be with you?
If we were both able

Wandering Thoughts

I'm here with him
But thinking of you
This just isn't right
But what else am I to do?

Is this deception?
I feel disgraced
I just miss you so much
And miss seeing your face

Would I be this way
If you were available?
Would I want to be with you
If we were both able?

4/27/08 12:22am

ILLUSIVE DREAM I.

② I can hear her trying to call me
③ my everything is moving in slow motion
① I'm coming, please hold on!
④ And I never make it there in time
for her to breathe.

she came to me in her time of need
And in my time of need as well
Things were falling apart in our Relationships
So we decided to rely on each other for help

After going through my drama
She asked, "where do we go from here?"
my memory and vision now so blurred
But my eyes and ears are not impaired

~~I never truly saw the vision of her~~
I just had a vision of her death
And can feel the strength of her cry

As she gasps or makes time for her last
breath
I'm struggling to ~~get to~~ reach her to save her life

I'm being haunted by these illusive
dreams..... Please wake me up!

82

Illusive Dream 1

'I'm coming, please hold on!'
I can hear her trying to call me
Now everything is moving in slow motion
And I never make it there in time for her to breathe

She came to me, in her time of need
And in my time of need as well
Things were falling apart in our relationships
So, we decided to rely on each other for help

After going through my drama
She asked, *'Where do we go from here?'*
My memory and vision now so blurred
But my eyes and ears are not impaired

I just had a vision of her death
And can feel the strength of her cry
As she gasps, one more time, for her last breath
I'm struggling to reach her, to save her life

I'm being haunted by these illusive dreams…please wake me up!

4/29/08 ✓

DELIVER ME

I feel like the devil's haunting me
When I haven't done anything wrong
I can have the best night with my family
Followed by a morning of slow song

Slow songs in my mind
Slow songs in my heart
It's the only thing that will jerk my tears
So I can have a better day with a fresh start

Why must I shed tears
And order to be happy again
Depression seems to be a high for me
And also the way the devil lets himself back in

I will fight him
And refuse his many advances
I will be happy with a cleansed soul
And with God will I take my chances

84

Deliver Me

I feel like the devil's haunting me
When I haven't done anything wrong
I can have the best night with my family
Followed by a morning of slow song

Slow songs in my mind
Slow songs in my heart
It's the only thing that will jerk my tears
So I can have a better day, with a fresh start

Why must I shed tears
In order to be happy again?
Depression seems to be a high for me
And also the way the devil lets himself back in

I will fight him
And refuse his many advances
I will be happy with a cleansed soul
And with God, will I take my chances

4/30/08 ✓

Mama's
~~Mommy's~~ Angel

The date is near
Of which you'd be a product of your father and I
Although you aren't here
You had to be of my illusion one more time

I saw you again last night
Just as beautiful as you were before
This time I held you and clutched you tight
Like I wanted you to stay a little while longer, just
a little more

I'd love for you to stick around
And keep my heart company
Together for life we will be bound
But people may start to think I'm crazy

They'll never understand what we have
As others would think we're insane
But you have to let me move on from my past
Because in my dreams you can't remain

~~If you loved me
you'll come to me one last time
tell me what you~~

Mama's Angel

The date is near
Of which you'd be a product of your father and I
Although you aren't here
You had to be of my illusion, one more time

I saw you again last night
Just as beautiful as you were before
This time I held you and clutched you tight
Like I wanted you to stay a little while longer; just a little more

I'd love for you to stick around
And keep my heart company
Together for life, we will be bound
But people may start to think I'm crazy

They'll never understand what we have
As others would think we're insane
But you have to let me move on from my past
Because in my dreams, you can't remain

Show me what you want me to see
Tell me what you want me to know
Before you make your journey for eternity
Give mommy a big kiss goodbye & have fun with
the angels

Show me what you want me to see
Tell me what you want me to know
Before you make your journey for eternity
Give mommy a big kiss goodbye, and have fun with the angels

5/4/08

May Fourth

Today is the 4th day
In the month of may
Don't have much to say
As I'm overwhelmed with dismay

① I was fine earlier today
② But found my thoughts going astray
④ Thinking things I dare not say
③ Tricks my mind seems to play

Father, lover, liar, deceiver..... hater.

May Fourth

Today is the fourth day
In the month of May
Don't have much to say
As I'm overwhelmed with dismay

I was fine earlier today
But found my thoughts going astray
Tricks my mind seems to play
Thinking things, I dare not say

Faker, lover, liar, deceiver...hater.

No Way Out

my job used to be my escape
now I can't stand it or the people
But I aint mad about what I make

my writing used to be my therapy
now it's just more work
Because now I stay angry

my home used to be my sanctuary
That lasted for all but a month
These days I'm lucky if it's even sanitary

Time used to be on my side
Now it's leaving me fast
And I continue to watch it go by and by

Time is also supposed to heal all wounds
But it seems to be taking forever
In result, I find myself always in a bad mode

my laughter used to help me
But now I haven't the strength for a chuckle
my anger supercedes my being happy

92

No Way Out

My job used to be my escape
Now I can't stand it, or the people
But I aint mad about what I make

My writing used to be my therapy
Now it's just more work
Because now I stay angry

My home used to be my sanctuary
That lasted for all but a month
These days I'm lucky if it's even sanitary

Time used to be on my side
Now it's leaving me fast
And I continue to watch it go by and by

Time is also supposed to heal all wounds
But it seems to be taking forever
In result, I find myself always in a bad mood

My laughter used to help me
But now I haven't the strength for a chuckle
My anger supersedes my being happy

5/8/08

If and When

③ If you love her
Don't be afraid to tell her

② If you've missed her
Don't be afraid to hold her

① If you like her
Don't be afraid to court her

④ If you need her
Don't be afraid to marry her

And when you do.....

Don't assume you're above her
As she is your equal

Don't lose the fire and desire for her
If you wouldn't want her to lose it for you

Don't let ya boys be your best friends
As they can't do the things she can do

Don't ever take her for granted
or the love she has for you

94

If and When

If you like her
Don't be afraid to court her

If you've missed her
Don't be afraid to hold her

If you love her
Don't be afraid to tell her

If you need her
Don't be afraid to marry her

And when you do…

Don't assume you're above her
As she is your equal

Don't lose the fire and desire for her
If you wouldn't want her to lose it for you

Don't let ya boys be your best friends
As they can't do the things she can

Don't ever take her for granted
Or the love she has for you

5/14/08

My Boo

Thank you for being you
no matter what we've been through

You keep me grounded
By your love I'm surrounded

you give me good sound advice
To where I never have to think twice

I love you whole heartedly
because our love comes naturally

You'll never have to guess what's on my mind
cause it's you all of the time

I don't have to tell you how I feel
cause in my thoughts, you're always appealled

My Boo

Thank you for being you
No matter what we've been through

You keep me grounded
By your love, I'm surrounded

You give me good sound advice
To where I never have to think twice

I love you whole heartedly
Because our love comes naturally

You'll never have to guess what's on my mind
Cause it's you, all the time

I don't have to tell you how I feel
Cause in my thoughts, you've always appealed

5/16/08

The Distance II

I'm hundreds of miles away
And I can't believe how much I miss you
To me, this almost never happens
Showing my feelings was always an issue

The Distance 11

I'm hundreds of miles away
And I can't believe how much I miss you
To me, this almost never happens
Showing my feelings was always an issue

5/25/08 ✓

Test the Theory

Ask anyone too many questions
They'll tell you at least one lie
no one is EVER going to volunteer information
Go ahead and give it a try

Do you love me
I sure do
But how much
Infinity times two

Test the Theory

Ask anyone too many questions
They will tell you at least one lie
No one is ever going to volunteer information
Go ahead and give it a try

'Do you love me?'
I sure do
'But how much?'
Infinity times two

5/28/08

Toxic Shock

day   You're my day cocaine
night   You're my night crack

day   I can't go through the day without saying hi
night   I can't sleep at night without you by my side

day   When we're not talking, we're playing hard to get
night   When we're not speaking you always tag ie forget

day   I'm always anxious to feel your touch
night   I love that you lust me as I lust you so much

day   I prefer you in the day, to stimulate my mind
night   I prefer you at night, to occupy my time

both   Neither one of you is better than the other
both   I'm just addicted to the constant high to keep it together

102

Toxic Shock

You're my day cocaine
You're my night crack

I can't go through the day, without saying hi
I can't sleep at night, without you by my side

When we're not talking, we're playing hard to get
When we're not speaking, you always forgive and forget

I'm always anxious to feel your touch
I love that you lust me as I lust you so much

I prefer you in the day, to stimulate my mind
I prefer you at night, to occupy my time

Neither one of you is better than the other
I'm just addicted to the constant high, to keep it together

5/30/08

Yelling the Truth

I almost feel kinda bad
I shouldn't have said what I said

But this is my idea of tough love
It wasn't a bit harsh, but it did make him budge

I thought I'd find a long email
Stating how loudly I whaled

To my surprise I found the opposite
I actually found nothing at all.

Yelling the Truth

I almost feel kinda bad
I shouldn't have said what I said

But this is my idea of tough love
It was a bit harsh, but it did make him budge

I thought I'd find a long email
Stating how loudly I whaled

To my surprise, I found the opposite
I actually found nothing at all

✓

Detached

Was that all it took?
for you to stop calling me
Was that all it took?
for me to stop being a need

Guess my bipolarism kicked in
And once again you're feeling the wrath
But when it's all said and done with
In the end I feel I chose the right path

Right path by purposely making you angry
knowing you don't like drama
Right path by hoping you no longer want to see me
So we both dodge the bullet of karma

So I ask you again
Was that all it took?
for our relationship to end
I guess we're now unhooked

That's all the whole; that's all it took
We're no longer together, and no longer hooked!

Detached

Was that all it took
For you to stop calling me?
Was that all it took
For me to stop being a need?

Guess my bipolarism kicked in
And once again, you're feeling the wrath
But when it's all over and done with
In the end, I feel I chose the right path

Right path, by purposely making you angry
Knowing you don't like drama
Right path, by hoping you no longer want to see me
So we both dodge the bullet of karma

So, I ask you again
Was that all it took
For our relationship to end?
I guess we're now unhooked

That's all she wrote, that's all it took
We're no longer together, and no longer hooked

I Hate my Life

I hate my life
I wish I could just end it
But the only reason I continue to strive
Is because I fear hell and its content

A simple slit of the wrist
And I could end it all right here
From me, no one would even expect this
And how they would feel, I really wouldn't care

I'm a selfish bitch
That needs to be alone
I'm feeling a bit lethargic
Slowly drifting away; soon to be gone

I might have taken a pill too much/many
So tell my family I love them all
When I no longer have a beat, do not resuscitate me
Just let me go, let me sink, let me fall

I Hate My Life

I hate my life
I wish I could just end it
But the only reason I continue to strive
Is because I fear hell and its content

A simple slit of the wrist
And I could end it all right here
From me, no one would ever expect this
And how they would feel, I really wouldn't care

I'm a selfish bitch
That needs to be alone
I'm feeling a bit lethargic
Slowly drifting away, soon to be gone

I might have taken one pill too much, many
So, tell my family I love them all
When I no longer have a beat, do not resuscitate me
Just let me go, let me sink, let me fall

*DISCLAIMER: These are just words and should never be taken literal. No one was hurt or harmed during the writing process of this literary work. Seek help through the Suicide Hotline if you're feeling this way. (800.273.TALK)

6/12/08 ✓

I Love My Life
Screw that, I love my life
And I'll be damned if I end it
The only 2 reasons I will continue to thrive
Is because I love both of my children

A simple slit of the whist
Could end it all right here
I tried and it hurts like shit
Besides hell; pain would be my other fear

I'm no where near selfish
And I can't stand being alone
I feel very much energetic
And not ready to go to the heavens called home

I'll never take any pill too much many
So I can tell my own family I love them all
No need to resuscitate me when I no longer have a beat
As I would've died of a natural cause

110

I Love My Life

Screw that, I love my life!
And I'll be damned if I end it
The only two reasons I will continue to strive
Is because I love both my children

A simple slit of the wrist
Could end it all right here
I tried and it hurts like shit
Besides hell, pain would be my other fear

I'm nowhere near selfish
And I can't stand being alone
I feel very much energetic
And not ready to go to the heavens, called home

I'll never take any pill too much, many
So, I can tell my own family I love them all
No need to resuscitate me when I no longer have a beat
As I would have died of a natural cause

*DISCLAIMER: These are just words and should never be taken literal. No one was hurt or harmed during the writing process of this literary work. Seek help through the Suicide Hotline if you're feeling this way. (800.273.TALK)

7/17/08 — **Still no Proposal**

It's been ~~6 yrs, 3mths & 163 days~~ — no we've been together
It's been 6 yrs, 3mths & 13 days that we have yet to get married
It's been 6 yrs, 3mths, & 13 days I can't believe that we haven't even set a date

After 6 yrs, 3mths, and 13 days do you think we still will be together?
After 6 yrs, 3mths and 13 days do you think we should be married?
After 6 yrs, 3mths & 13 days do you think we will ever _____?

Even these 2,293 days I've put up a whole lot of shit
Even these 2,293 days _____ put up with a whole lot of shit as well

When this long period of time you give me nothing to _____ used to
Over this long period of time, you've given me nothing but empty promises

When does it begin for us to be a family
When does it begin for us to be where we should've been as a family?
When is the _____ going to be more just _____ than friends
When are we _____ friends and lovers

Still No Proposal

It's been 6 years, 3 months and 13 days that we've been together
It's been 6 years, 3 months and 13 days that we've yet to get married
It's been 6 years, 3 months, 13 days and one child later that we haven't
even set a date

After 6 years, 3 months and 13 days do you think we should still
be together?
After 6 years, 3 months and 13 days do you think we should
get married?
After 6 years, 3 months, 13 days and one child later do you think there'll
ever be a date?

Over these 2,293 days, I've put up with a whole lot of shit
Over these 2,293 days, you've put up with a whole lot of shit as well
Over this long period of time, you give me nothing to look forward to
Over this long period of time, you've given me nothing but empty
promises

When does it begin for us to be a family?
When does it begin for us to be where we should've been as a family?
When is the wait going to be over?
When are we going to be more than just friends and lovers?

8/5/08 :)

The muse I.

my muse is gone
I've lost my fire
I have no more to complain about
As the love is gone for the one I once desired

I don't need him anymore
As he no longer inspires me
He's disrespected me for the last time
With all his slick talk and vulgarity

The game is getting old
And I'm tired of going along with it
I've waisted so much time on this fool
That I've been taking my own man for granted

It's easy for fools to tell you to leave
With no conscience of how you'd survive
Because it's always about them & their needs
not about you and how that change will affect your life

114

The Muse 1.

My muse is gone
I've lost my fire
I have no more to complain about
As the love is gone, for the one I've once desired

I don't need him anymore
As he no longer inspires me
He's disrespected me for the last time
With all his slick talk and vulgarity

The game is getting old
And I'm tired of going along with it
I've wasted so much time on this fool
That I've been taking my own man for granted

It's easy for fools to tell you to leave
With no conscience of how you'd survive
Because it's always about them and their needs
Not about you, and how that change will affect your life

8/7/08

Wannabe Jump off

I thought of him all day long
wondering when he's going to call
Or send me an email to say hi
But I got not one word at all!

It's now the afternoon
2. And what do I get
A text saying hi
Perhaps from the one I suspect

No, but of course not
4. It's from the one I want to forget
why won't he just leave me alone
And forget that we ever met

We've never had relations
5. not even a mere Kiss
no emotions shared what-so-ever
not even moments shared to miss

All this time texting
3. Before I knew a name
I knew it wasn't my night crack
So it had to be my day cocaine

116

Wannabe Jump Off

I thought of him all day long
Wondering when he's going to call
Or send me an email to say hi
But I got not one word at all

It's now the afternoon
And what do I get
A text saying hi
Perhaps from the one I suspect

All this time texting
Before I knew a name
I knew it wasn't my night crack
So it had to be my day cocaine

No but of course not
It's from the one I want to forget
Why won't he just leave me alone?
And forget that we ever met

We've never had relations
Not even a mere kiss
No emotions shared what-so-ever
Not even moments shared to miss

It was neither my crack
nor my day cocaine
It was the wannabe jumpoff
whom has become to be a pain

118

continued

It was neither my crack
Nor my day cocaine
It was the wannabe jumpoff
Who has become to be a pain

8/7/08 ~1

Broken Routine

I can't help but to think about him
As he was part of my daily routine
Came to work clock in and then we'd chat
But now I only see him in my dreams

He is still of this world
Yes, very much alive
I just chose a different path
And the right one for my life

He's called me three times
But not at all to speak
He wants me to know that I'm on his mind
By calling & hanging up on me

I understand his methods
As I've done them myself
However, I don't plan on giving in
Or asking him for any kind of help

Usually in really hard times
I'd call him for gas money
In which he's going to want something in return
Which is why I don't even bother calling

120

Broken Routine

I can't help but to think about him
As he was part of my daily routine
Come to work, clock in and then we'd chat
But now I only see him in my dreams

He is still of this world
Yes, very much alive
I just chose a different path
And the right one for my life

He's called me three times
But not at all to speak
He wants me to know that I'm on his mind
By calling and hanging up on me

I understand his methods
As I've done them myself
However, I don't plan on giving in
Or asking him for any kind of help

Usually in really hard times
I'd call him for gas money
In which he's going to want something in return
Which is why I don't even bother calling

8/21/08

Thank your Parents

~~Thankin off of the escence of you~~

You're everything I've ever wanted in a man
As cliche' as that may sound
I've wished and dreamed for someone like you
Someone me to love me and turn my world around

I'm high off of the very essence of you
So much that I feel like thanking your mother
She's raised a smart, fine and vibrant man like yaself
with star qualities making the perfect lover

The lover who likes me inside & out
The lover who can't wait to be around me
The lover who makes me laugh out loud
The lover who has the potential to heal my soul & rescue me

122

Thank Your Parents

You're everything I've ever wanted in a man
As cliché as that may sound
I've wished and dreamed for someone like you
Someone to love me, and turn my world around

I'm high off the very essence of you
So much, that I feel like thanking your mother
She's raised a smart, fine and vibrant man like yourself
With star qualities, making the perfect lover

The lover who likes me, inside and out
The lover who can't wait to be around me
The lover who makes me laugh out loud
The lover who has the potential to heal my soul and rescue me

8/29/08

Possible keeper

Although we've just met
I feel like you already know me
I'm always so anxious to hear your voice
Because it calms me, so gently

It's been such a long time
Since I've felt this way
I can't explain how happy I am
And we've only met that once on memorial Day

Perhaps you are what I've waited for
maybe... just maybe you are my change
The change I've been looking & longing for
The change that's perfect for me and just my age

I say just my age
Because you're just my type
you can sing, dance, and play basketball
Do all the things that I like.

All I want is to see you again
So I can get lost ~~when~~ ~~we can~~ ~~so it can~~
~~then pick up there~~ ~~and again~~
So we can pick up where we left off
Then I can get lost in your rapture
And
So we can begin what we never started

124

Possible Keeper

Although we've just met
I feel like you already know me
I'm always so anxious to hear your voice
Because it calms me, so gently

It's been such a long time
Since I've felt this way
I can't explain how happy I am
And we've only met, that once on Memorial Day

Perhaps you are what I've waited for
Maybe…just maybe, you are my change
The change I've been looking and longing for
The change that's perfect for me, and just my age

I say just my age
Because you're just my type
You can sing, dance and play basketball
Do all the things that I like

How?

How do I tell him,
That I don't want to do this anymore?

How do I tell him,
That I still love him, but need more?

How do I tell him,
That I want to be happy?

How do I tell him,
That he isn't the one for me?

How do I tell him,
To let me go so I can be?

How do I tell him,
To be alone, single and free?

How do I tell him,
That I want to be away from the drama?

How do I tell him,
That I fear the future contents of his karma?

How?

How do I tell him
That I don't want to do this anymore?

How do I tell him
That I still love him, but need more?

How do I tell him
That I want to be happy?

How do I tell him
That he isn't the one for me?

How do I tell him
To let me go so I can be?

How do I tell him
To be alone, single and free?

How do I tell him
That I want to be away from the drama?

How do I tell him
That I fear the future contents of his karma?

Acknowledgements

For the second time around, God remains to be first and foremost on my list to thank for giving me the continued strength to put together another book for all my wonderful readers.

Ah yes, my wonderful readers…I appreciate the love you steadily show me on this roller coaster ride of emotions in the *Poetry in the Raw* book series. It is guaranteed to pique your curiosity with who are you, who am I, and what is raw? If you haven't figured it out by now…

It is everything you've just read,
With plenty more that will be said,
If you stick with me, there's more to come,
This is book two, so don't forget to get *Authentic*, book one.

Last and certainly not least, to The Margo6. I love you all for showing me constant love and support through what I went through then and who I am now.

About the Author

Photo by Jason Cordes Photography

Ciara Dove was born and raised in Passaic, New Jersey. She is the third child on her mother's side and one of many siblings on her father's side. In 1995, her literature teacher told her she had great writing skills which empowered Ciara with a passion for writing. While she did take a hiatus from writing, in 2006 she felt as though inspiration reignited in her soul and she wrote over 300 poems.

Facebook.com/AuthorCiaraDove/

TikTok: @authorciaradove

Instagram: @authorciaradove

Stay in-tuned with these current and upcoming titles
in the *Poetry in the Raw* series by Ciara Dove.

Available Now!

AUTHENTIC
ORGANIC

Coming Soon!

NOSTALGIC
ARCHAIC
BONA FIDE
PRIMAL

www.ingramcontent.com/pod-product-compliance
Lightning Source LLC
Chambersburg PA
CBHW060937120626
46557CB00003B/1027